ORKNEY FROM OLD PHOTOGRAPHS

ORKNEY
FROM OLD PHOTOGRAPHS

Selected by
GORDON WRIGHT

With an introduction by
BRYCE WILSON

GORDON WRIGHT PUBLISHING
55 MARCHMONT ROAD, EDINBURGH, EH9 1HT
SCOTLAND

ISBN 903065 36 3

Printed and bound by Clark Constable Ltd., Edinburgh.

CONTENTS

Acknowledgements   6

Introduction   7

                                                    Illustration Number

The Orcadian Photographers   1-6

Early Photographs   7-14

The Orkney Family and Home   15-27

Kirkwall   28-46

Stromness   47-60

Around the Mainland   61-72

Around the Islands   73-83

Fishing   84-98

Farming   99-115

Transport   116-132

Craftsmen and Tradesmen   133-142

Traditions and Customs   143-147

Leisure   148-157

Orkney Folk   158-179

Miscellany   180-195

ACKNOWLEDGEMENTS

My sincere thanks to Bryce S. Wilson, Museums Officer for Orkney for writing the introduction, helping to research photographs and caption many of the illustrations. Without his expert advice it would have been impossible for me to compile this book.

Mr. Stanley Horne for his kindness and generosity in allowing me free access to his father's collection of photographs, therefore allowing a most expensive production to appear cheaper than would have otherwise been possible.

Mr. David Tinch, A.L.A., Librarian and staff at the Orkney Library, Kirkwall.

Stromness Museum (Orkney Natural History Society).

Tankerness House Museum, Kirkwall.

The Scottish Dept., Edinburgh Central Library.

Mr. Robert N. Smart, Keeper of Manuscripts, University Library, St. Andrews, for information on the photographs of J. Valentine.

Aberdeen University Library, for information on the photographs of George Washington Wilson.

Dr. Derek Johnstone, Stromness, for helping me to locate Mr. John Nankivell and his unique album of old Orkney photographs.

Photographs which appear in this book were supplied as follows.

The numbers which appear after each name refer to the photographs in order of appearance.

Mr. Stanley Horne: 5, 20, 21, 23, 24, 26, 27, 28, 35, 39, 40, 41, 42, 43, 44, 45, 65, 85, 88, 91, 99, 101, 103, 104, 105, 106, 108, 109, 110, 111, 113, 122, 123, 127, 128, 139, 141, 148, 150, 151, 152, 153, 154, 155, 156, 157, 166, 169, 171, 172, 183, 184, 191, 194, 195.

Tankerness House Museum, Kirkwall: 3, 17, 25, 29, 32, 33, 46, 73, 74, 76, 96, 100, 114, 115, 131, 138, 140, 144, 173, 174, 175, 178, 182, 186.

Mr. W. A. S. Bews: 4, 55, 56, 57, 58, 59, 64, 67, 69, 94, 98, 118, 121, 124, 126, 137, 142, 146, 164, 167, 170, 185.

Mr. John M. Leonard: 19, 34, 36, 37, 68, 70, 71, 79, 80, 102, 112, 125, 133, 159, 160, 188, 192.

Stromness Museum: 7, 14, 83, 84, 92, 97, 117, 120, 163, 165, 189, 190.

Mr. Gordon Wright: 1, 38, 61, 66, 75, 86, 130, 136, 145, 161, 162, 187.

Mr. John Nankivell: 15, 48, 49, 50, 51, 52, 53, 63, 116, 149.

Mr. Peter Leith: 54, 72, 93, 107, 119, 132, 134, 181.

Mr. Bryce S. Wilson: 9, 10, 12, 13, 16, 62, 135.

Mr. Edgar Muir: 8, 60, 87, 89, 95, 168.

Edinburgh City Libraries: 18, 22, 77, 90.

The Orkney Library, Kirkwall: 78, 82, 147.

James Grant & Co. (Highland Park Distillery) Ltd.: 30, 31, 129.

Mr. William Wolfe: 47, 193.

Mr. George Mackay Brown: 176, 177.

Mrs. B. M. Walthew: 11, 158.

Mr. Kenneth Foubister: 81.

Mr. Bruce Gorie: 143.

Mr. Alistair Cormack: 180.

Mr. James Brown: 179.

Miss Edith Wood: 2.

Mr. Allan: 6.

GORDON WRIGHT

INTRODUCTION

The first photographic print was made in 1826 by a French lithographer and inventor, Joseph-Nicephore Niepce. In 1839 his partner, Louis Daguerre, revealed the first practical photographic process, and the field was open for exploitation.

It is not known when the first photographs of Orkney were taken; perhaps among the earliest are two tantalisingly distant views of Kirkwall and Stromness included in the 1867 edition of Barry's *History of Orkney*. Other early prints have survived, their faded sepia preserving the ghosts of long demolished buildings in familiar streets, with stove-hatted businessmen and moleskin-trousered labourers pausing to assist the photographer in a long exposure.

By the 1860s, Orcadians were having their portraits taken. Long the preserve of the upper classes who could afford the services of portrait painters, this was made widely available in the mid-19th century through photography, especially the cheap 'ambrotype'. The process involved no printing. The glass negative, with a little colour tinting to the cheeks and clothing of the sitter, was given a black background of paper, paint or even soot to render a positive image. It was enclosed behind glass with a pretty frame of thin gilt brass, then placed in a wooden velvet-lined case covered in imitation tooled leather. Ambrotypes can be found throughout the islands, and one can imagine a band of happy young folk queueing for their 'likeness' beside an itinerant photographer's tent at the Lammas Market.

By 1875, W. H. Wood had set up as a part-time photographer in Finstown, and five photographers are listed in the 1890 edition of *Peace's Orkney Almanac*. Soon the great Family Bible was joined in the Orkney home by an equally impressive looking volume — the Family Album.

The development of photographic 'views' paralleled portraiture. Two of the best-known firms of commercial photographers in Scotland, G. W. Wilson and J. Valentine, sent photographers to the islands to capture the awe-inspiring in cliff scenery and the picturesque in narrow streets and ancient farmsteads. The march of science which accelerated change in slow moving island life also provided the means of recording it.

Here they all are; the farmer confronts a harvest field with sickle or scythe; a farm girl drags a huge wooden rake to glean straw. Others burn kelp by a lonely shore, or flash knives over herring by a harbour crammed with fishing-boats. It would be easy to romanticise these scenes; to forget the unending, back-breaking toil, the stench of burning kelp and fish-guts, the over-crowding of many homes, and the poverty of many of the people.

Orkney photographers also took to recording the local scene, perhaps as a welcome relief from 'bread-and-butter' portraiture. Among these, Tom Kent was outstanding. From his studio and shop in the Broad Street of Kirkwall (now occupied by The Longship) he recorded the passing of the old order and the emergence of the new. Among other gifted and enthusiastic photographers in Orkney were R. H. Robertson, David Horne, and a little later, Willie Hourston.

The photographers of the 19th and early 20th centuries made a great many original prints for sale, and booklets of 'views' were published. By 1890 the picture postcard was established as a popular collector's item, and yet another impressive volume, the Postcard Album, entered the household.

The preoccupations and pastimes of the Edwardian era were interrupted by the 1st World War, and gradually the old albums were consigned to dusty attics. The cumbersome glass plates of the early photographers became old-fashioned with the advent of cheap box cameras and roll film. They had remarkable powers of survival, however, if left undisturbed in lofts and garden sheds, but they gradually diminished as now and then a store was cleared out or demolished. The murky rectangles of glass, of no apparent interest, were consigned to the quarry or the harbour; a few were occasionally put to use in the garden to shelter plants!

Another war passed. Then came the 1950s and a new prosperity. The increasing mechanisation of post-war life changed the world considerably, and people began to look back with nostalgia to 'the good old days'. Here and there, around the country, old negatives would be unearthed, to reveal a fascinating world distanced by time. Horse-drawn vehicles, sailing ships, elaborate fashions, a host of trades and occupations which had disappeared. Plates were reprinted and admired. Further caches were unearthed, exhibitions mounted and books published. Family and postcard albums were bought up at auctions or snatched from the brink of bonfires.

By a stroke of great good fortune for Orcadians, the majority of Tom Kent's glass plates had been preserved, and now form the basis of the photo archive at the Orkney Library. Other collections which have survived include the plates of R. H. Robertson, W. H. Wood, David Horne, Willie Hourston and George Ellison, an annual visitor from Liverpool at the turn of the century, whose plates have been presented to Stromness Museum. In addition, small collections of the plates of other photographers turn up from time to time. Many of these have been loaned or presented to the Orkney Library, where they are printed and filed and made available for public use. The Library adds to this by re-photographing old prints loaned by members of the public. These include 'snapshots' taken on the family box camera which, although lacking in artistic and technical merit, often have unique subject-matter.

This book will be welcomed by many at home and abroad, giving as it does a lively cross-section of the remarkable photographic record available to Orcadians.

Bryce S. Wilson
17 September 1981.

1.   A Monitor whole plate camera manufactured by the Rochester Optical Co., Rochester, New York. The lens is a 6 ins. Cooke Primoplane, Series V11A. with a f6.5 — f45. aperture. Exposure by lens cap. Owned by Tom Kent of Kirkwall. (Tankerness House Collection) (*Photo: G. Wright*)

W. H. W. WOOD

PHOTOGRAPHER

FINSTOWN,

ORKNEY.

NEGATIVES KEPT

COPIES CAN BE HAD ANY TIME

The Orcadian Photographers

2. William Hugh Wood

3. Tom Kent

4. Robert Heddle Robertson

5. David Horne

6. William Hourston

William Hugh Wood was born in Curcabreck, Rendall in 1830. He was employed as postmaster in Finstown after his father-in-law Joseph Johnston.

He was possibly the earliest commercial photographer who stayed in Orkney, and from examples of his work which have survived it seems he was particularly interested in portraiture.

It is not known when he started taking photographs, but assuming that he had started by the time he was forty, then he was at least in business in the 1870s, possibly earlier.

There are ambrotypes in existence dating from the 1860s which could possibly have been taken by him (Joseph Mowat of Graemsay (P. 15) for example).

William Wood was brought up in the same parish as Tom Kent, so we can assume that they knew each other. In fact, when Tom Kent emigrated to America he was accompanied by Wood's son David.

William Wood died on 30 July 1903 at the age of seventy-four.

Tom Kent was born in Firth in 1863. He emigrated to the U.S.A. as a young man, where he worked in a Chicago drug store and it was there that he developed an interest in photography. He returned to Orkney in 1897 and in 1898 he opened a shop in Albert St., Kirkwall and set up as a photographer. He then moved to better premises in Broad St. where he also sold photographic accessories, books, stationery and fancy goods. There is evidence that he did well, owning a thriving business, a car, and he made many friends among the landed gentry in Orkney at the time.

Tom Kent was a first class photographer. He utilised the most sophisticated equipment available at the time and working with a large format negative produced well defined images which were technically excellent. Combined with his own artistic ability which was considerable, he produced a wide variety of photographs recording life in the Orkney Islands over a period of thirty odd years.

Many of Tom Kent's landscape and seascape compositions provide fascinating detail, while his group shots and individual portraits prove his ability to obtain the necessary response from his subjects at the right moment to bring his photographs to life.

In spite of a largely successful career, it seems he fell on bad times, and when he died on 11 August 1936 at the age of seventy-three, the event passed almost unnoticed.

His large photographic legacy will always remain a most important part of Orkney's heritage.

Robert Heddle Robertson was born at Grutha in South Ronaldsay in 1872. He moved to Stromness in the late 1890s at the height of the herring fishing boom, and opened two grocers shops, one in Alfred St. and one in Victoria St. which also sold photographs and photographic equipment.

During the fourteen years he lived in Stromness he continued to indulge in his hobby of photography on a semi-professional basis which included producing photographic post cards which he sold in his shops.

Lack of trade caused by the decline of the herring industry made him leave Stromness in 1912 to take up the position of manager of the Westray Co-operative. He continued to take photographs for the best part of his life and died in 1963 at the age of ninety.

David Horne was born in Kirkwall in 1877 and shortly before his father's death he took over the family business of David Horne, bacon curers, who had their premises and retail shop in Mounthoolie Lane, Kirkwall.

David Horne's interest in photography was purely as an amateur and although his coverage was mostly limited to his native Kirkwall and surrounding districts, he captured many interesting aspects of his time neglected by other photographers.

Working with a small format plate camera $4\frac{1}{4}'' \times 3\frac{1}{4}''$ he produced his best results and several hundred of his photographic plates have been preserved by his family in good condition.

He was also a talented writer of both prose and poetry and he contributed regularly to several newspapers and magazines. He was also extremely interested in the antiquarian lore of Orkney and was a valued member of the Orkney Antiquarian Society.

David Horne died in 1940 at the age of sixty-three.

William Hourston was born in Evie in 1895. When he came to Stromness in the 1930s he ran a billiard saloon and barber shop in the ground floor of the building which is now the museum.

He took up photography and recorded the raising of the German Fleet which had been scuttled in Scapa Flow. He had an unfailing eye for the beautiful view and the newsworthy picture, and his early training as a joiner enabled him to make his own enlarger and much of the ancillary equipment which he used so well in his work.

As time passed, photography took up more and more of his time. His calendars were a feature of the Christmas season with views of the countryside and the sea in all its moods and always with an appropriate sky-scape.

For a time he was an occasional lighthouse keeper on Sule Skerry, one of the more isolated stations thirty miles into the Atlantic, west of Orkney. It was the haunt of sea birds and seals, all of which he recorded with his camera.

He served in both great wars. He was a gunner in France and was the sole survivor of the crew of a howitzer which exploded, receiving injuries which affected him all his life. In the more recent conflict he was an N.C.O. in the Territorial Army serving in various batteries in Orkney.

William Hourston continued taking photographs until the late 1950s. He died in Stromness in 1968.

Early Photographs

7. An ambrotype, believed to be Joseph Mowat of Graemsay, who was drowned on 1st. January 1866 while helping to rescue passengers and crew of the ship *Albion* which had grounded on Graemsay at the Point of Oxon. (*Photo: unknown*)

8. The ship *Lady Head* of the Hudson's Bay Company in Stromness Harbour. During the 18th and 19th centuries Orkney supplied a large proportion of the fur-trading company's work-force in Canada. The ships ceased calling in 1891. (*Photo: unknown*)

9. Home on leave? An unknown Orcadian Hudson's Bay man. c. 1870. (*Photo: Wm. Wood*)

10. Four stalwarts photographed in the photographer's studio at Finstown, c. 1870. (*Photo: Wm Wood*)

11. Graemshall, Holm, seat of the Graeme family. The House of Meall in the left foreground probably dated from the late 15th century; the block behind was built in 1626 by Bishop George Graham. The whole complex was demolished in 1874 to make way for the present Victorian mansion. c. 1870. (*Photo: unknown*)

12. A mother poses with her three children. c. 1870. (*Photo: Wm. Wood*)

13. Four Orcadian dandies enjoy a glass of ale. c. 1880. (*Photo: Wm. Wood*)

14. The Rev. Dr. Charles Clouston of Stromness and Sandwick. A noted amateur of science, he was the first President of the Orkney Natural History Society which founded Stromness Museum in 1837. He kept weather observations in his parish from 1827 until his death in 1885. (*Photo: unknown*)

The Orkney Family and Home

15. A prosperous looking family gather outside their greenhouse. c. 1880. (*Photo: unknown*)

16.   This cottage near Finstown, which appears to be newly built, shows clearly the method of covering a flagstone roof with straw ropes or 'simmens' to protect it from the elements. It also has fireplaces in the gables instead of the traditional central hearth. c. 1870. (*Photo: Wm. Wood*)

17.   Skaill House in Sandwick dates back in part to the early 17th century when it was the seat of Bishop George Graham whose arms are above the main door. It has been much enlarged since this photo was taken in the late 19th century. It is now a listed 'A' building of outstanding interest. c. 1889. (*Photo: J. Valentine*)

18. Feolquoy, Stromness, one of the last Orkney houses with a central hearth. c. 1900. (*Photo: T. Kent*)

19. A woman grinding with a hand quern. Behind her are a wooden yoke for carrying buckets and a heather besom. c. 1900. (*Photo: T. Kent*)

20. This old farm house in Stronsay has a flagstone roof covered in simmens. The adjoining barn has the traditional grain drying kiln. c. 1900. (*Photo: D. Horne*)

21. Washing day at a country cottage. c. 1905. (*Photo: D. Horne*)

22. The interior of Netherby, Deerness. With a few notable exceptions the central hearth, a feature of Orkney houses from earliest times, died out during the 19th century. The room contains the basic necessities; box beds with sliding doors, meal girnels, straw-backed 'steuls' and spinning wheels. c. 1900. (*Photo: T. Kent*)

23. Carrying home water with an iron hoop to steady the pails. c. 1905. (*Photo: D. Horne*)

24. Farm children at play, 1914. (*Photo: D. Horne*)

25.   A family at work cutting peat, the staple fuel of the islands. c. 1900. (*Photo: T. Kent*)

26.   The family stand proudly before a new stone built dwelling at 'Rosebank' in Stronsay. c. 1904. (*Photo: D. Horne*)

27. A family enjoy a picnic in the lea of a dry stane dyke. c. 1905. (*Photo: D. Horne*)

Kirkwall

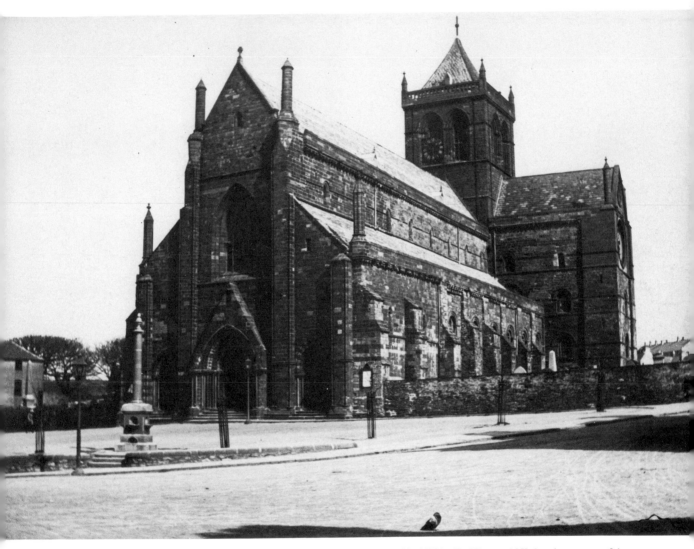

28. St. Magnus Cathedral 'the wonder and glory of the North', was founded in 1137 by Earl Rognvald Kolsen in memory of the martyred Earl Magnus. The low spire in this photograph was replaced by a higher one during restoration in 1919. (*Photo: D. Horne*)

29. Demolition in Broad St., Kirkwall. The house on the left was built by Harry Erburie. One of Cromwell's soldiers, Erburie stayed in Kirkwall and became a prosperous merchant and bailie of the town. The house on the right was built in the late 17th century by Margaret Grott, widow of Patrick Prince, merchant. c. 1884. (*Photo: unknown*)

30. Highland Park Distillery, Kirkwall, was founded in 1798. This photograph was taken from the west in 1888. (*Photo: unknown*)

31. Highland Park Distillery Still House as it was from 1920-63. (*Photo: unknown*)

32. The Big Tree of Albert St., Kirkwall, when it was enclosed in a private garden. When the corporation wanted to widen the street and applied to purchase the private ground, the conditions of sale stipulated that they should retain one tree. c. 1870 (*Photo: unknown*)

33. Albert St., Kirkwall. c. 1889. (*Photo: J. Valentine*)

34. The Basin, Kirkwall Harbour. Earldom rents from the North Isles (paid in kind) were landed at the Corn Slip in the foreground. c. 1900. (*Photo: T. Kent*)

35. The Merkat Cross, Kirkwall. Dated 1621, it was situated at the foot of the Strynd, the old market place of Kirkwall, before being moved to the position of the present replica cross. The original cross is now housed in St. Magnus Cathedral. c. 1900. (*Photo: D. Horne*)

36. The Lammas Market, Broad St., Kirkwall 1923. Thousands of people converged on Kirkwall from all over Orkney for the three day Lammas Market, Orkney's principal livestock sale. The main attraction, however, lay in the merchants' booths and amusement stalls on the Kirk Green. (*Photo: T. Kent*)

37. Good natured banter assists a sale by auction in Broad St. at Kirkwall Lammas Fair in 1923. (*Photo: T. Kent*)

38. Bridge St., Kirkwall, 'Where two wheelbarrows tremble when they meet' c. 1900. (*Photo: T. Kent*)

39. Cleaning the windows of Irvine's boot shop, Victoria St., Kirkwall. c. 1900. (*Photo: D. Horne*)

40. Mr. Twatt, tailor, Kirkwall. c. 1900. (*Photo: D. Horne*)

41. Sunset on Kirkwall Harbour. c. 1900. (*Photo: D. Horne*)

42. This view of Kirkwall from the West shows the original extent of the Peerie Sea, now much reduced by reclamation. c. 1900. (*Photo: D. Horne*)

43. The old Kirkwall Grammar School. T. S. Peace's fine 19th century building has been preserved as the offices of the Orkney Islands Council. c. 1905. (*Photo: D. Horne*)

44. Cyclists in procession on Palace Rd., Kirkwall. c. 1900. (*Photo: D. Horne*)

45. The British Torpedo Flotilla in Kirkwall Bay, photographed from the tower of St. Magnus Cathedral, August 1906. (*Photo: D. Horne*)

46. A parade of Free Masons during peace celebrations in Kirkwall 19 July 1919. (*Photo: T. Kent*)

Stromness

47. A traditional Orkney 'yole' ties up at one of the many small piers (now known as Flaws's Pier) in Stromness "the Venice of the North", 1909. (*Photo: F. Cuthbertson*)

48. At Leask's Corner in Stromness, a woman pauses in the laborious task of carrying coal in a creel on her back. The close on the left is still called Pigeon Creek. c. 1880. (*Photo: unknown*)

49. The Pier Head, Stromness, before the building of Mackay's Stromness Hotel, the Harbour Office and the Customs House. c. 1880. (*Photo: unknown*)

50. Miller's Close, John St., Stromness. The house is dated 1716 and has been occupied continuously by the Miller family. c. 1880. (*Photo: unknown*)

51. Victoria St., Stromness, with the old Mason's Arms Hotel on the right. c. 1880. (*Photo: unknown*)

52. Stromness Distillery, founded in 1828, produced the well-known 'Old Orkney' whisky. It closed in the 1930s. The site is now occupied by Mayburn Court housing scheme. c. 1880. (*Photo: unknown*)

53. Fish for sale at the foot of Church Rd., Stromness. c. 1880. (*Photo: unknown*)

54. Sam Stockan, Stromness Town Crier, taken on the occasion of Queen Victoria's Diamond Jubilee in 1897. (*Photo: unknown*)

55. The 'Hurdy Gurdy Man' with his barrel organ and monkey near Melvin Pl., Stromness — one of a number of travelling entertainers who visited the islands early this century. c. 1900. (*Photo: R. H. Robertson*)

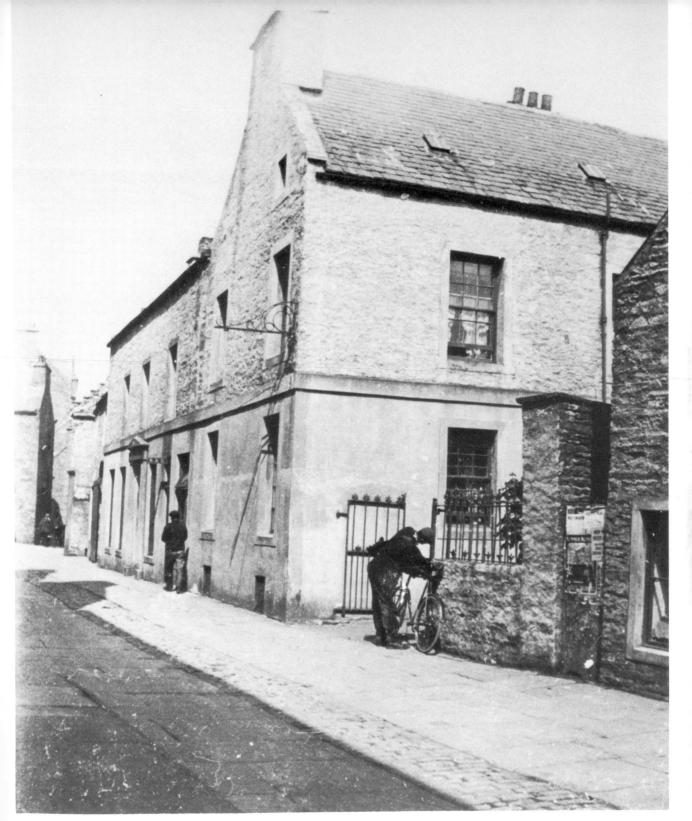

56. The Mason's Arms Hotel, Victoria St., Stromness, now the Oakleigh Hotel. c. 1900. (*Photo: R. H. Robertson*)

57. John Johnston, better known as 'Soldier John', Town Crier of Stromness in the early years of this century. c.1900. (*Photo: R. H. Robertson*)

58. Temperance workers outside R. H. Robertson's grocer shop in Alfred St., Stromness. c. 1900. (*Photo: R. H. Robertson*)

59. J. Rae, bookseller, Victoria St., Stromness, was also agent for a number of shipping lines catering for emigrants. c. 1900. (*Photo: R. H. Robertson*)

60. Stromness in winter from Millburn. c. 1900. (*Photo: unknown*)

Around the Mainland

61.   The Dounby Show, 13 August 1908. As always, a highlight of the Orkney social calendar. In the foreground, a shop van belonging to James Flett, baker, Finstown. (*Photo: unknown*)

62. John Firth's joiner shop, Finstown. John Firth, author of *Reminiscences of an Orkney Parish* is standing on the left with his wife and daughter. c. 1870. (*Photo: Wm. Wood*)

63. Relaxing at the Ring of Brodgar, Stenness, c. 1880. (*Photo: unknown*)

64.   Postal workers at Sandwick. c. 1900. (*Photo: R. H. Robertson*)

65. Gathering 'spoots' (razor fish) during a 'spoot ebb' at Scapa. 1905. (*Photo: D. Horne*)

66. The village of Birsay, known as 'the P'lace' after the ruined palace of the Stewart earls. c. 1900. (*Photo: T. Kent*)

67. W. B. Firth's shop van from Stenness, on the Back Road, Stromness, with the newly constructed villa 'Redroof' in the background. These travelling shops served the country districts from the late nineteenth century. c. 1900-10. (Photo: R. H. Robertson)

68. Finstown from the old Kirkwall Rd. c. 1900. (*Photo: T. Kent*)

69. A family of tinkers at Stromness. The tinkers travelled the countryside making and mending tin pails. c. 1900. (*Photo: R. H. Robertson*)

70. Old houses at Houton, Orphir. c. 1900. (*Photo: T. Kent*)

71. Unveiling the War Memorial at Holm, 5 September 1920. (*Photo: T. Kent*)

72. Excavating the Stone Age village of Skara Brae. Left foreground — Professor V. Gordon Childe who was responsible for the excavations. c. 1920. (*Photo: T. Kent*)

Around the Islands

73. Rackwick on the Island of Hoy. In the 19th century the valley supported a community of crofter-fishermen. Now almost deserted, it is a favourite haunt of summer visitors. c. 1889. (*Photo: J. Valentine*)

74. *S.S. Orcadia,* Orkney Steam Navigation Co., plied to the North Isles of Orkney from 1868-1931 from Kirkwall. c. 1880. (*Photo: G. W. Wilson*)

75. *S.S. Fawn,* passenger boat (1892-1917) calling at Rousay Pier. c. 1900. (*Photo: T. Kent*)

76. St. Margaret's Hope, South Ronaldsay, from the east. c. 1880. (*Photo: G. W. Wilson*)

77. Cutting peats on the Island of Hoy. c. 1889. (*Photo: J. Valentine*)

78. A windmill used for grinding grain at Peckhole, North Ronaldsay. c. 1900. (*Photo: T. Kent*)

79.   Whitehall Village, Stronsay. The village grew and flourished during the herring fishing boom of the 19th and early 20th centuries. c. 1900. (*Photo: T. Kent*)

80.   The Ferryhouse, South Ronaldsay. c. 1900. (*Photo: T. Kent*)

81. The Mill of Bea, Sanday — now demolished. Water mills of this type served the needs of every island and parish. (*Photo: K. Foubister*)

82. Landing goods on Papa Westray. c. 1900. (*Photo: T. Kent*)

83. The lighthouse on the Pentland Skerries, 28 December 1914. The twin towers were built in the 1820s to replace Robert Stevenson's earlier towers first lit on 1st. October 1794. The lantern on the lower tower was replaced by a foghorn in 1909. Donkeys were kept to transport supplies from the boat to the tower. (*Photo: unknown*)

Fishing

84.   Herring boats leaving Stromness Harbour for the fishing grounds. During the late 19th and early 20th centuries, the Scottish herring fleet used Orkney as a base in early summer and numerous curing stations were established. c. 1900. (*Photo: unknown*)

85. J. S. Foubister, Newbanks, Deerness, baiting the handlines for haddock fishing. Orcadians traditionally depended on the sea for a large part of their diet. c. 1900. (*Photo: D. Horne*)

86. A Birsay fisherman carries buoy-ropes for lobster creels and a wand for 'cuithe' fishing. c. 1900. (*Photo: T. Kent*)

STROMNESS IN FISHING TIME.

87. During the six weeks of the herring fishing season in early summer, Stromness harbour was crammed with as many as 300 boats and every pier bustled with the activity of herring gutters and packers. c. 1900. (*Photo: unknown*)

88. A Fifie fishing boat sets sail from Kirkwall harbour. c. 1900. (*Photo: D. Horne*)

89. The fishing fleet leaves Hoy Sound in pursuit of the herring shoals. c. 1900. (*Photo: unknown*)

90. After a day at sea the Rackwick fishermen arrive home with their catch. c. 1889. (*Photo: J. Valentine*)

91. Steam drifters unload their catch at Kirkwall harbour. c. 1906. (*Photo: D. Horne*)

92. Andrew Young, an apprentice cooper at More's yard in Stronsay. Many coopers were employed making barrels for the salt herring which was then exported to the industrial towns of Britain, as well as to Ireland, Russia and Germany. c. 1920. (*Photo: Chas. Chalmers*)

93. Herring gutters at the Warehouse Pier, Stromness. c. 1920. (*Photo: Wm. Hourston*)

94. Salting and packing herring into barrels at Ness, Stromness. c. 1900. (*Photo: R. H. Robertson*)

95. Sunday was a day of rest for coopers and gutters, many of whom followed the herring fishing around the country. c. 1900. (*Photo: unknown*)

96. Packing dried fish at Chalmers fish store, Ayre Rd., Kirkwall. c. 1900. (*Photo: T. Kent*)

97. Fisher folk in Stromness. c. 1900. (*Photo: G. Ellison*)

98. Fish salesmen at Stromness. c. 1900. (*Photo: R. H. Robertson*)

Farming

99. Farming is traditionally the most important activity in Orkney. In this harvest scene near Kirkwall the farmer cuts oats with a back delivery reaper, which began to replace hand shearing in the islands in the late nineteenth century. c. 1900. (*Photo: D. Horne*)

100. An iron plough yoked to a pair of oxen, Hoy. c. 1880. (*Photo: G. W. Wilson*)

101. Scything and gathering crops at Deerness. c. 1905. (*Photo: D. Horne*)

102. The back-breaking 'charlie' rake was used to glean straw from the harvest field. c. 1900. (*Photo: T. Kent*)

103. These hand threshing mills began to take over from the flail from around the 1850s. c. 1900. (*Photo: D. Horne*)

104. Marking a pig for market. c. 1900. (*Photo: D. Horne*)

105. Before the widespread use of fencing, cattle were herded daily in the summer hill pastures by children. c. 1907. (*Photo: D. Horne*)

106. Watering horses at a spring. c. 1900. (*Photo: D. Horne*)

107. Two milking cows pulling a clod-crusher, a simple flagstone with the 'operator' standing on top to provide extra weight. c. 1900. (*Photo: T. Kent*)

108. Singling turnips at Deerness. c. 1905. (*Photo: D. Horne*)

109. Feeding the hens. c. 1910. (*Photo: D. Horne*)

110. Breaking up ploughed soil with spring-toothed harrows. c. 1900. (*Photo: D. Horne*)

111. Harvesting with a two-wheeled reaper. c. 1900. (*Photo: D. Horne*)

112.   Rooing a sheep. The fleece would be spun and knitted to clothe the family or woven into blankets. c. 1900. (*Photo: T. Kent*)

113.   'Staigie Monday' at the Crafty in Kirkwall, where stallions or 'staigs' showed their paces before being put to stud around the islands. The site is now occupied by the Phoenix Cinema car park. c. 1900. (*Photo: D. Horne*)

CARTING HAY IN THE ORKNEYS

114. Forking hay onto a four wheeled Orkney 'sled' in Rackwick, Hoy. c. 1920. (*Photo: Wm. Hourston*)

115. Part of a stackyard of W. G. Rendall, Skaill, who won first prize and medal in a stackbuilding competition in 1929. The stacks are bound with simmens. (*Photo: T. Kent*)

Transport

116.   A most unusual cycle combination. c. 1880. (*Photo: unknown*)

117. *S.S. Express* was built at Shields for George Robertson to operate the Pentland Firth crossing from Scrabster to Stromness 1869-77. (*Photo: unknown*)

118. *R.M.S. St. Ola* 1. the passenger service steamer which operated between Scrabster and Stromness 1892-1951. (*Photo: unknown*)

119. An ox and cart on the Island of Hoy. c. 1880. (*Photo: G. W. Wilson*)

120. Transporting a load of herring barrels. c. 1890. (*Photo: unknown*)

121. A Shetland pony harnessed in Stromness. c. 1900. (*Photo: R. H. Robertson*)

122.   Setting off from Deerness to do some shopping. c. 1905. (*Photo: D. Horne*)

123.   A family gig outside Charlie Robertson's grocer shop in the High St., Kirkwall. c. 1905. (*Photo: D. Horne*)

124. Couper's coach in Whitehouse Lane, Stromness. c. 1900-10. (*Photo: R. H. Robertson*)

125. Six-in-Hand, Kirkwall. c. 1900. (*Photo: T. Kent*)

126. The Post Office trap outside the old Post Office in Alfred St., Stromness, which was closed in 1903. L. to R. — Wm. Rendall Jnr., George S. Robertson, (later Postmaster and Provost of Stromness. He died in 1981 at the age of ninety-four), unknown, Wm. Rendall Snr. (he also ran the printing press in Stromness), unknown, Mrs Ross, Postmistress and James Couper. c. 1900. (*Photo: R. H. Robertson*)

127. The Orkney Motor Express No. 1, leaving Harbour St., Kirkwall for Stromness. c. 1900. (*Photo: D. Horne*)

128. The first car in Orkney at MacLennan's Office, Kiln Corner, Kirkwall. c. 1900. (*Photo: D. Horne*)

129. Unloading coal onto a lorry from a steamer at Kirkwall Pier to fire the stills of the Highland Park Distillery. c. 1910. (*Photo: unknown*)

130. The opening run of the Orkney Motor Club to Dounby, 18 April 1913. (*Photo: T. Kent*)

131. The first motorbike and sidecar in Kirkwall. L. to R. Tom Rosie, Agnes Delday, Michael Morgan, Betty Delday and John T. Reid. c. 1920. (*Photo: T. Kent*)

132. An early aeroplane at Cumminess, near Brig o'Waithe. Aberdeen Airways landed in a field near Stromness in the 1930s. (*Photo: Wm. Hourston*)

Craftsmen and Tradesmen

133. Shoeing a horse, the Orkney blacksmith also served as farrier. c. 1900. (*Photo: T. Kent*)

134. Geordie Garrioch, the village smithy at Finstown. c. 1890. (*Photo: unknown*)

135. You need strong teeth to make a straw caisie. Used in the barn or for carrying peat. c. 1900. (*Photo: Linklater*)

136. Mr. Kirkness of Kirkwall making a straw-backed Orkney chair. c. 1900. (*Photo: T. Kent*)

137. Stone masons dressing flagstones for the construction of Stromness Lighthouse Pier. c. 1900. (*Photo: R. H. Robertson*)

138. Hugh Bain, weaving homespun in Westray. c. 1900. (*Photo: T. Kent*)

139. A tinsmith working in Kirkwall. c. 1905. (*Photo: D. Horne*)

140. A formidable steam roller in Kirkwall. c. 1900. (*Photo: T. Kent*)

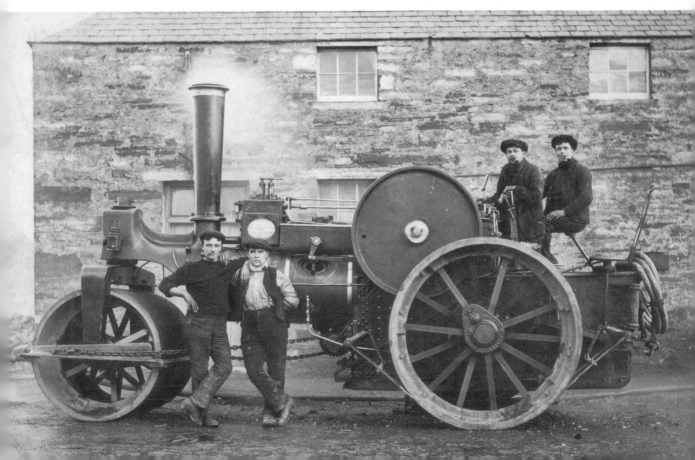

141. Quarry workers at Deerness. c. 1900. (*Photo: D. Horne*)

142. Carpenters at work extending Stromness Academy. c. 1905. (*Photo: R. H. Robertson*)

Traditions and Customs

143. Weighing children on the pundlar. An old Orkney Christmas custom to see how much a child had increased in weight throughout the year. c. 1870. (*Photo: unknown*)

144. Starting off on 'the walk' at an Orkney wedding. Traditionally the bridal party and guests walked from the bride's home to the church or manse for the ceremony and returned there for the celebrations. c. 1890. (*Photo: Linklater*)

145. A tense moment in Broad St., Kirkwall, during the traditional New Year's Day Ba' game of 1907. The game is played at Christmas and New Year between 'Uppies' participants born above the Post Office Lane, and 'Doonies' those born between the Post Office Lane and the Harbour. (*Photo: T. Kent*)

146. Thomas Rendall 'swappan for aaks' in Westray. Wild fowl made a welcome supplement to the islanders' diet. c. 1912. (*Photo: R. H. Robertson*)

147. A Hallowe'en prank at Millhouse, Deerness. c. 1900. (*Photo: T. Kent*)

Leisure

148. Paddling in Kirkwall Bay at Ayre Mills. c. 1900. (*Photo: D. Horne*)

149. A Victorian Sunday afternoon near the Double Houses, Stromness. c. 1880. (*Photo: unknown*)

150. Collecting bait on a rocky shore, 1919. (*Photo: D. Horne*)

151. Putting in the streets of Kirkwall. c. 1900. (*Photo: D. Horne*)

152. A walking race during sports at Bignold Park, Kirkwall. c. 1900. (*Photo: D. Horne*)

153. A display of fashion as three ladies pose on the roof of St. Magnus Cathedral. Centre, Mrs. David Horne. 1905. (*Photo: D. Horne*)

154. The Ducky Pond, Kirkwall. It was later drained and the Infant School built on the site. c. 1900. (*Photo: D. Horne*)

155. Two friends enjoy a fill of tobacco. c. 1900. (*Photo: D. Horne*)

156. The photographer's wife poses with a parasol. 1912. (*Photo: D. Horne*)

157. The Cheerful Chums Jazz Band of Kirkwall. L. to R. Barrie Brass, Jeannie Horne, Edith Miller, Stanley Horne and David Horne Jnr. "Cubbie Roo" of the *Orkney Herald*, 1927. (*Photo: D. Horne*)

Orkney Folk

158. The family and their retainers at Graemshall, Holm. c. 1870. (*Photo: unknown*)

159. "Tillie-illie-arum", a Kirkwall boot-maker. c. 1900. (*Photo: T. Kent*)

160. Annie Harper, a spae-wife from Rendall. c. 1900. (*Photo: T. Kent*)

161. Johnny Wood the elder. c. 1900. (*Photo: unknown*)

162. William Laughton "Skatehorn", a wandering eccentric of the turn of the century. (*Photo: T. Kent*)

163. Five Orkney Heroes. L. to R. Robert Reid, William Burgar, James Groat, John Hercus and John Drever, five North Fara men who saved the crew of the Peterhead trawler *Hope* on 28 December 1908. They were presented with ten pounds each by Dr. Andrew Carnegie. (*Photo: T. Kent*)

164. An old sea-dog. c. 1900. (*Photo: R. H. Robertson*)

165. Nellie Newlands, the highly respected matriarch of a large family of tinkers who plied their trade throughout the islands. c. 1920. (*Photo: Wm. Hourston*)

166. Mr. and Mrs. J. S. Foubister, Newbanks, Deerness. c. 1900. (*Photo: D. Horne*)

167. Kirk outing from Graemsay to the Orkney mainland. Back Row L. to R.: Daniel Sutherland, Sandside; James Mowat, Horn; Jean Mowat, Horn; Jessie Sutherland, Sandside; Agnes Sutherland, Sandside; Hughina Mowat, Hill; Kitty Linklater, Fillets; Isabella Wilson, Nether Newhouse; Kitty Sutherland, Sandside; Bill Skinner, Quoys.
Middle Row L. to R.: Hugh Lyon, Clett; Cissie Lyon, Breckan; Catherine Jane Sutherland, Sandside; Kate Scott, Hoy Low Lighthouse; Mr. Fraser, Church of Scotland Missionary; Maggie Mowat, Hill; Mary Jane Skinner, Quoys; Kate Anne Lyon, Breckan; John Henry Wilson, Nether Newhouse; Joe Mowatt, Ramray.
Front Row L. to R.: George Sutherland, Sandside; Janet Scott, Hoy Low Lighthouse; Kitty Lyon, Clett; Magdalene Mowatt, Ramray; Ina Mowatt, Ramray; Kitty L. Skinner, Quoys; Alice Linklater, Fillets; James Wilson, Flaghill. c. 1908.
(*Photo: R. H. Robertson*)

168. Moments of contentment. c. 1900. (*Photo: unknown*)

169. Miss Mary Peace of Kirkwall in evening dress. c. 1903. (*Photo: D. Horne*)

170. Stromness Lifeboat *John A. Hay* and crew. Standing L. to R.: Robert Greig Snr., coxswain, James Johnston, Mr. Budge, James Robb, James Thomson, Robert Gunn and W. Nicolson. Seated L. to R.: Robert Greig Jnr., James Leask, William Johnston and S. Anderson. 1909. (*Photo: R. H. Robertson*)

171. Mr. David 'Porky' Horne, bacon curer and pork butcher, Mounthoolie Lane, Kirkwall, many of whose photographs appear in this book. 1922. (*Photo: D. Horne*)

172. "What's wrang wi' ye the day Porky Horne?" Four youngsters at the back door of David Horne's shop after being chased outside for coming too near the cutting equipment used for dividing carcasses. 1920. (*Photo: D. Horne*)

173. Right: Edwin Muir, the distinguished Orcadian poet.

174. Bottom L: Stanley Cursiter, painter, and subsequently the Queen's Painter and Limner in Scotland.

175. Eric Linklater: novelist.
c. 1920. (*Photos: T. Kent*)

176. George Mackay Brown and his elder brother 'Norrie' sail their model yacht from the rocks at Stromness, 1925. (*Photo: Wm. Hourston*)

177. Infants 1 Class at Stromness Secondary School in 1927. Three notables are George Mackay Brown, middle row extreme left. Ian MacInness, the present Rector of Stromness Academy, holding the slate. Mr. Jim Robertson, proprietor of Robertson's Confectionery factory at Stromness, third from left, front row. (*Photo: Wm. Hourston*)

178. Tom Kent at work photographing a cist grave. c. 1930. (*Photo: unknown*)

179. Four pairs of great-grandparents at East Bigging, Yesnaby. L. to R.: Mr. and Mrs. Bremner, Forswell, Yesnaby; Mr. and Mrs. Brown, Croval, Sandwick; Mrs. Brown and James, East Bigging, Yesnaby; Mr. and Mrs Harvey, Iverach and Mr. and Mrs. Linklater, Skaill. c. 1939. (*Photo: Wm. Hourston*)

Miscellany

180. A horse-drawn hearse used in Sanday until just after the second world war. It was used for funerals from the North End which had a considerable journey to reach the Lady Parish cemetery which is in the centre of the island. (*Photo: A. Cormack*)

181. Burning kelp at Breckness near Stromness. Kelp was burned to produce iodine and potassium salts, used in the manufacture of glass. On the left is James Leask, better known as "Puffer", the well-known Town Crier of Stromness. The women are Maggie Allan and her two daughters. c. 1889. (*Photo: J. Valentine*)

182. This snap-shot from Westray shows two balls of straw ropes or 'Simmens'. These were made in winter for roofing and binding stacks. (*Photo: Unknown*)

183. Deerness Parish Church, c. 1900. (*Photo: D. Horne*)

184. The North Transept, St. Magnus Cathedral, before restoration. c. 1905. (*Photo: D. Horne*)

185. The wreck of the trawler *S.S. Sunbeam* at the Black Craig, Stromness, 1905. (*Photo: R. H. Robertson*)

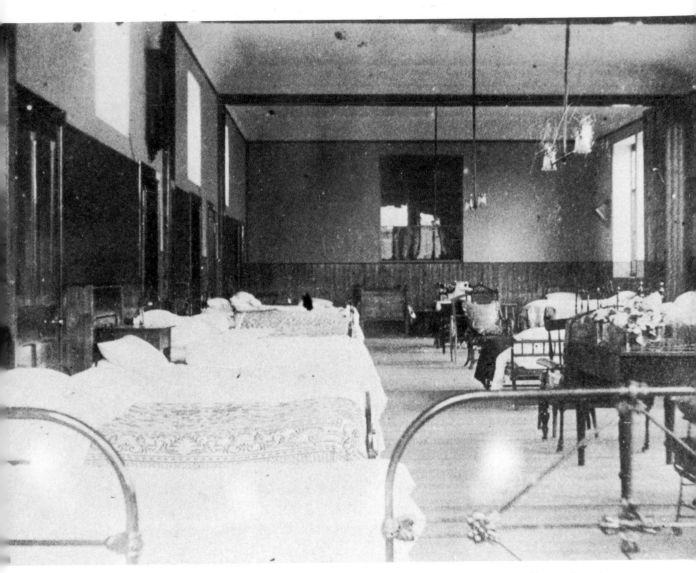

186. Emergency hospital beds set up in Kirkwall Grammar School during the 1914-18 war. (*Photo: unknown*)

187. The German Fleet interned at Scapa Flow after the First World War. 28 November 1918. (*Photo: T. Kent*)

188. The Germans scuttled their fleet on 21 June 1919. These destroyers were grounded on Fara. (*Photo: T. Kent*)

189. Salvage operations on the German Fleet in the 1920s. (*Photo: Wm. Hourston*)

190. *S.M.S. Hindenberg* was salvaged by Cox and Danks Ltd. in 1930. (*Photo: Wm. Hourston*)

191. A 70 ft. whale grounded at Deerness in 1905. (*Photo: D. Horne*)

192. One of the bells of St. Magnus Cathedral, removed temporarily during restoration work early this century. c. 1914. (*Photo: T. Kent*)

193. Two tourists, James Henderson and Tom Wolfe are 'put off the island' after a visit in 1909. (*Photo: F. Cuthbertson*)

194. "Oh for the touch of a vanished hand and the sound of a voice that is dear." 1903 (*Photo: D. Horne*)

195. A new generation, 1900. (*Photo: D. Horne*)